SEBASTIANE, 1976

*in tribute to the homoerotic theory that
died on those rocks for love*

I have cast myself in this poem
as Jarman's Sebastian, in order to give
credence to the notion that
everything in this book happened to me

an arrow-pierced and bleeding
hawk with a spat out tooth, a saint
with the sky in my mouth

filigree green
delicate as nothing spider
I was never

so lonely as I was
when I was loved
by my oppressor

The men laugh
and bite each other's thighs
their pissing silhouettes
against the sky like gods
painting sun on muscle

I close my eyes
water drips from my beard, through my lips
my nipples, down my ass

I tense to depict
my suffering through movement
2-dimensional
a flat elegance

To be disgusted in the company of others
autocrat of myn
own loneliness
a seagull crying in a storm

I reach my shell arm to the air
its tilting tiers, pearlescent
scintillans I can feel
resentment growing
at the edges of their joy

LIGHT FILM

LIGHT FILM
Sholto Buck

The Contents

★

I throw swords in a pile
a lyre I kneel
to sip the pearl
plucked from sea
and wreathed upon the rocks

My foe fucks on mythical
ground, wrestling
in the gush of waves
the sun bounces off
my armour and my red thong
dressed

for orgiastic combat
against brethren for refusing
my commander's desires
wield
the cut stone
of zeal

Sparkling droplets spiral
this violence feels theatrical

Cadmium thick
pig's blood painted on the sand

Salt ration, silver coin
cup of dice, idle
soldier fingering
the knife's edge

I whisper into
my jailer's open mouth

You don't need to go on
You don't need to rub that mineral cream

I unsheathe his boot
laurel crown
spat wine
I think about lips

Your laugh like an invisible hand
reaching down your mouth your hand
is tearing out your heart

From the love I didn't want
I know that I will die

lying with my mouth closed

It happens in slow-motion
coral ribbons run down

If I have regrets
like in the movies

my ass, perfect no matter what
curves against the sea

I take my breath
the archers take their place

THE SOUND OF RAIN IN A CLEAR SKY

When I was a child, I spent
a lot of time finding ways to stop
objects from touching the ground.

Some high foot, a parachute
and so on. My gestures,
gay in the way things often are.

I arch my back
in approximation of a perfect curve. Purring,

all sound is acoustic
each surface artificial.

There is a score that blots the windshield.
There are carlight reflections on the road like crying eyes.

I decide what's real.
The wave of my hair, this bright drop

the word around my closing fist.

WATCHING A BURNING HOUSE

I thought I could burn boredom from me.
But it rained.

I was
annoyed.

For one so disciplined
I was silver melting

with every move I made

leaves turned x-ray coloured
blew toward me in divided wings.

It wasn't a tragedy.
I created this problem.

ARROWS POINTING UP / ARROWS POINTING DOWN

I always fail
in love with liars,

plastic, mustard
I want this

fantasy to be
gratuitous as I am

pleasant when I gag
some handsome

armpit, turned
on like a lamp

light like a thin
dumbbell, the sky

sweating does
get darker than

this, coffee with milk
my life is going to change

TEOREMA, 1968

A winter scene: I lie in bliss. You stand
over me, a shirt in the shape of a man.
White briefs on the floor.
This is an allegory told in clothes
and the bodies that empty out of them.
Cigarette ash falling on a bulge.
Your spread wide tight
cream pants and sadness in your eyes.
I frame your luscious glance in perfect
clean glass. A white glove on a hairy ass.
Kiss the saint and then the star.
No history could reflect this truth. What's real
is fantasy. The memory of a thing
that didn't happen. In the factory the bosses slacken.

I WANT TO BE IN LOVE AND NEVER STOP CRYING
I WANT TO FEEL TO THE POINT OF BLINDNESS

Everyone has a limit
to the dreams they can make come true.

I mean
the landscape

walked
a red
spiral of green

through me.
I held its flame in my palm.

IT IS, AFTER ALL, IMPOSSIBLE
TO BE TAKEN SERIOUSLY

This burger wasn't for crying
into but I ate it whole
I want arms as long
as the metal arm that crushes cars
I want to be better
than that man's handsome face
better than the book
I was not
content with
oblivion
when it came
trimming the hem of my pants
this hallway wasn't lonely
until I threw myself out of it

I CREATED THIS PROBLEM
THEN I WROTE IT ON A CRACKED SCREEN

gemmed bulge
 exploding egg
jellied fake
smell of paper
what time does
a painting
almonded
 dead

MONOLOGUE

When light touches you Sholto you are touched by nothing.
The lilacs transforming toward you—
The spider of your hair in sunlight—
It's not a tragedy
light burns your face. It can't
kill you. Your sacred
way of seeing
nothing. A cruel bull
plunged a horn in you. How beautiful
you were, how light
the fence that divides
reality from your dreams.
You hold your axe
against the summer.
You claim to feel
more acutely than others.
This always happens.
You look at me
and I look at you.

WITHOUT DIALOGUE THERE IS SURFACE

(a long driveway)

    (the bejewelled waist of a man)

                    (double helix)

          (dressed lilies)

(blood on a clean suit)

      (the lushest green)

           (rats asleep like commas on the grass)

        (wet pedestrians float off)

(a rained on zebra crossing)

      (piss run down a leg)

          (the hot shadows of towels)

        (photographs of the scandal)

(almond coloured satin)

    (rose-petaled) (chain on an oiled wheel)

         (a cotton veil pulled over the arm of a chair)

        (curved fantasia)

(fur in pale dust)

      (the bluest part of a night)

ON A DIFFERENT SCREEN

We play the game whose rules are fake

Chop your purply thwacking scowl!
Fuzzy downs the crying fowl!

But what does it say about love?

Here,
stand on this platform

Here,
a stilt for every fool

RABBIT'S MOON, 1972

The film is supposed to be over, but the score is still playing
I am watching rain replace the heat outside

A popped balloon, I play it back
a little in my head

Satan walks through a glass door
A face slides against itself

Concentric, a clown
I am binding

my finger to the moon
fling me

from it to the clear
coloured glass and paper cutout forest

I thought this
feeling was a cliff

Double orgy, cefalexin, hell
bent upon a satin rag

I march stage left and stretch
then turn away, hold the pose

And that's life: arms hanging
awkward to the fake sky

In my living room
the air conditioner is broken

and a mutual acquaintance
is hitting on my boyfriend

on Grindr
I am wondering

about the health of my gut relative to the health
of everyone else's guts

Tinsel hangs
forlorn as anything

Falling is righteous
it approaches holiness but fails

to become itself instead
the rain

outside is getting in
my living room window

KNIFE + HEART, 2018

In which I star as me:
the actress on the verge of tears.
Neck arched like a swan, lilting
synth or barn on fire. This is

my swelling password
protected aria, I'll tell anyone

you broke my heart.

In the nightness of my mood.
In the stare of a genital's eye.

I'm on a quest
for mystery. Chemical,
your slagging jaw
slow as a winding tape.

Switch / delete / death
into its perfect

theatre
a muscly thick

alchemy that spits
back what I know

I ran away
but even then

I woke up running.
Toward a telephone in an empty room.

Blue chandelier into red right angle
corridor. In the film,
you killed me.

Eye bored into parted lips.
Ornate,
my sailor outfit in the grass.

Kiss the mirror.
Jerk off slowly.

My belt, a sculpture of clasping hands.
This language is my only secret.

A slow arriving train and the fire of memory
burns into me like a negative. Here lies

my masterpiece: the long cinema
of obsession:

I was paradise's
burning son.

Fire fighting was an Olympic sport
and I starred as myself

in every crisis.

IT WAS NICE, YOU WERE DAMAGED

a relieved wailing
a wave

      a clungungungung

collapsible cardboard
boxes click

      on nasal key

still drawn here
from casualty I turn

you don't really love the world

then flat fall off the sea

             in another
                life
               I was
     your thudded sharp and blunting

              pretty shore

PULLING A SAUSAGE FROM A FORK
WITH MY TEETH

I will never lift
the sadness I was born with
a plain sensation

BODY CREAM

Lubed up
in scabies medication
I eat my porridge in the rain
well-mannered as a baby
I could be
your charismatic party guest
when our conversation uncurls
like a limit, sweetheart
I say your name until I can't
see you / I say
finger me
like the 19th century
doctor treats hysteria / I am not
your woman patient, I'm
a water sign
and there is nothing more to know
about a person than the sound
of their name, and I can love
any perfume
so long as I hate it first

ALL NIGHT I LAY IN THE WET HEAT IMAGINING BEING STRUCK BY LIGHTNING

I read an article about perfumes inspired by snow
I make a piece of toast

the crust, so chewy as I bite
my body breaks
in
on itself I don't know why
I am starting yet to cry
how my love has made me lie

JORDAN'S DANCE, 1977

This is a formal experiment in violence, addressed
to the joke of purity. She dances
against pleasure. Nature, entropy, dereliction, fat.
The tutu and the garbage fire. Diaphanous
heat exudes from each and both imply the swift
collapse of beauty. This loss is inept
to the expression of grace that is
our birthright. Wet dirt. Standing under
a bridge. Linear shadow,
slow-motion bounce. Ash floats
through the air like moths.
What we might call urban. A muscly guy
wearing a Greek mask on his face. The word carnivalesque,
the burning Union Jack. It makes me think
of Leda and the Swan, she is playing
both parts. Whirling bright,
catastrophe. A minimal
and brutal costume, I see it
coming apart.

PEPPERMINT FRAPPÉ, 1967

A sliced kiss magazine face.
Eyelash lacquered cream liqueur.
Lampshade, the shape of ice.
I draw myself into a file.
I fold myself on seafoam glass.
That's me, running down
stairs like an ethereal girl. 1, 2, 1, 2
klonopin, red fabric and glue.
An index finger pressed into a nose.
Clean shaven, image like a slick
incising force. A wound band.
Leaves on concrete; leaf
on a rained-on windscreen. I've seen
every frame, nothing can destroy me.

FROM LOVE I WENT LOOKING

Ecstasy, my little tease
hold me from the fire please

cut the garter from my thigh
when I say I want to die

drag your thumb along the hem
of my underwear and then

kiss me slow, turning key
leapt the word back into me

like a coin tossed in a well
from your sunburned hand I fell

hard upon the earthly ground
to the ruin where I found

when I want to have my way
paradise, the hell I say

THE HOUR OF THE STAR, 1985

1

face like an idiot
chalicing
I'm not afraid of words
knowledge with enough
sugar to vomit

a creamy soup
a statue filled with gold
to live inside
a name, its grammar
I have gorged

solitude, a truer wealth
it ruined my life and gave me everything I wanted

2

in a beautiful storefront
my sadness is a dirty star

reasonless, I ride the train
pose like a mannequin

I think men are cruising me
but they are blind or telling me to move

I sit on a bench with this stupid
giant orange embarrassment

3

what a shocking flock of doves
day leaves me

a yellow t-shirt riding away

[AND LET IT DOWN]

love screamed through my life
leaves, the lushest green

from my translucent shield
I've floated

I swear

it held my flame in its palm
and let it down

THEATRE OF WRATH

In love
with what divides—I am one

who plays to lose. The ideal
masculine passive: when fucked

he sees his beauty mirrored.
Alive

in double solitude, my single
free arm reaches for a flower.

To be adored is the height of manliness.
Arms, bulged as a swan

Biblical blah blah, desire
made of lack. A pattern

of linking knocks. My hard-on
pressed against the wall. I suck

through reeds of straw. I'm becoming
myself. I'm coming

alone and it doesn't
end. A poem

is a visual medium, like men
wrestling naked.

LOVERS REHEARSE THEIR FINAL SCENE

1.

We moved like images

I should say

the image is a sickness of light

2.

An image petaled. It was my own
sickness and it burned
you?

3.

Like a swollen sick, my hope burned me.

You came, and I swallowed.

4.

Should pain
petal over me?

To be wrong is moving
yet
was I of sorrow?

5.

Light

moves

pooled

in the field of your lovely face.

6.

My love! Hate placed me
in wrongness, a sorrowed field.

I face it
over and over, a sickly pool.

To be the swollen moon, fucked.

7.

You placed a petal on my pain. Love swallowed me.

THEOREM, 1968

I am going to tailor my trousers and fuck
so many similar-looking men
to remember what it felt like
to kiss your hairy face. This is a futile quest
but what isn't. Concrete
platforms laid like a chess board.
I will make my life with what you left.
A footprint of a cloud on sand.
I will go where you might see me.
Standing around, the kind of thing
that happens every day. My love
killed me into a dream
and left me there. My silk tie
thrown down from a balcony.

A QUIET DINNER

I left your house at 10:30

you were nice
to tell me that my tongue was clean

I wanted to say that

you have the face of a childhood pet
but not mine

> your tan chest
> creasing at the edge
> as heavy luggage does
> drag on gravel in the middle of the night

I wake up crying
it was just an idea

I DIDN'T GET THE JOB, MY RENT INCREASED, I BROKE UP WITH MY BOYFRIEND, TESTED POSITIVE FOR CHLAMYDIA

or

AUTUMN LIGHT

At the Melbourne Sexual Health Clinic
I cry opposite the unfashionable
gay guy couple waiting together.
I make their intimacy my own
emergency. It's ok
to want it to hurt. I think
blonde people are the most vulnerable
to bad lighting. I decide that
I am in a deep connection with my community.
I'm excited to see how
love changed me, now that I'm not
in it. On the train,
a woman's dress is printed with the word
MYSTERY, repeating
on an angle. It's sacred
to accept risk; I have to live
inside the images I write to demonstrate pain.
A tattoo of a Birkenstock sandal
passes by. The good feelings don't last.
I walk around, sit illegally
in the outside section of a chain
sushi restaurant, and let the sun infect me
with vitamins. I am medically sensitive
to light this week, because of the drugs
for the chlamydia I'm treating
as a grounding experience.
Every day I'm better, I say
what happens has tremendous force.
Yesterday, a stranger asked me
did I make up my own name.

SHOLTO KIND OF RHYMES WITH SORROW

This pleases me in a way that means
something. I have been told

to get a life. Is suffering
temporary? Like love

has no limit. A bee sting precedes
an identical zit. I can perceive

a narrative structure in pain. No
I don't think

beauty will make me better.
When I see an empty field, I walk

into the middle of it.

IT WAS SO DARK AND INTENSE, BUT JUST A NARROW BAND

falling asleep in april
sunlight, I hear my mother
as a voicemail
driving through rain

PLACE A DROPPED COIN ON YOUR WINDOW, AS I LEAVE

a bee lands like a flower
on the narrow corner of my eye
eat a panful of cacio e pepe, feel
a real sensation
toward a single point
nausea's loop
threads me through it
pepper trees in the sun
the train's yellow
font drives back
I stumble
flu-sick, smile at strangers
dissolve the object
I focus on
Jewell Station under construction
seafoam ribbons of caution
tape / the sky / what I say
aloud is less
than half the gold / I want
the little scratches on my gums
from using your toothbrush

THEY SAY IT IS NIGHT I SAY IT IS MORNING

I'm in a disappointing position.
Every time I need someone they're like
aw palm tree! And run through a door.

Strained to a high pitch,
an emoji of the moon.
I lick trouble. Time, I mean

pulls prayer into a stupid shape.
When it comes it goes, a low siren
ringing like a snake

about to bite. Cutlery arrives
from nowhere. Fur-lined boots.
I hear the words
leggy lesbian ha ha ha,

this pattern of indecent sense.
A hard mirage of sound. Well
is still a chance I say
when hope bucks.

NARCISSUS LOOKS FOR WORK

Part 1) I was known for having huge triceps

When they turned me into a flower
I disputed reason

with an idle that could only be described
as gorgeous

I took a hundred personality quizzes
and was the opposite of each result

To imply the presence of my body
I wrapped the cord of a lamp around my thigh

Part 2) Gazing at my reflection was an act not of vanity but fitness

Naked in sunlight, I stood
at a window watching traffic.

I denied the feeling of a day
as a productive unit of time.

I went shopping.

Freight ships came and went.
I watched them from tall steps.

The night grew still.
I turned toward it.

I sat in bed with my laptop balanced on my knee
and stared at the sleeping screen. When I breathed,

my lapel curved like the petal of a lily.

SLEEPING PILL

I move from room to room, noticing small shifts
in temperature. I write
on my hand the word
Gallantry
in cursive loops. I jerk off
to men's faces
rolling like a credit sequence
on my phone.
I look up, what is
Time in LA
Shingles rash
Sofia Coppola net worth.
The night smell
of rained on jasmine.
When I walk outside
the street looks exactly
like itself. My heart goes
mute. To the quietest part
of a mind, the world will reach
like a waving hand
I'm passing through my life.

IN THE DREAM I HAD AFTER YOU, ONE HAND TOUCHED ANOTHER. A SHIRTSLEEVE SWUNG THROUGH EMPTY SPACE.

Psychedelic, sequinned orange
fabric on the wall.
Am I normal enough for the room?
You are not in it. I'm looking at fruit
painted on the window and trying
to be less combative with these normie guys
I want to fuck. None of them are like you.
At this gay club, I am the funniest person.
My dentist told me that
when he took out my wisdom teeth
I bled the standard amount.

MIRROR, 1975

I walk out across the marsh. Wet green
peace. The leaves blow back
their clinking lace.

In summer, I would swim in this river. Confetti
floating on glass. I let silence wash me.

I'm trying to decide if there's such a thing
as an absolute feeling.

I doubt it. When I say your name
in my mind, an oily film.
I do still think about you

turning from a white flame. Language
was absent in the way
we left it.

I look straight ahead, it is a clear morning in the place I live
think, I've never been here.

FIRE ISLAND

Before the orgy, a friend told me he cried
watching Derek Jarman's My Very Beautiful Movie.
I was sitting on his bed, slowly taking off my shirt.
I embarrassed myself then, saying declaratively
that I hadn't seen it and movies do not make me cry.

My friend laughed. I've been known to fall
in love with what pushes me. An attempt
to cross boundaries, a poem, a wedge
of light sliced in the dune.

The film is six minutes long, and I watch it
in the Melbourne Airport without sound, so I can write
about my life. On the screen, a thin man is naked
on the beach, a starfish curling

in his hand. The image looks like water
pooling in an eyelid. A warping piece of glass
and the slope of his hard shoulder. The star

is a porous shell. Shattered
piles of wood on sand. He makes
a shape with his elbow. His leg,
silhouettes into a dick.

Gays come to fire island to look at water,
and to participate in orgies. A story
that's been told. My face reflects
on airport glass and back

to the wooden ruin, the part of the sand that is a border
between wet and dry. I am concentrating
on what's in front of me. This horizon is
a flat and definite reality.
A shelf you could lean an arm on.

The wool of a wave flows in. I pause on
his speedo in the sand. The starfish rests
between his lips and thumb, counterpoised
by the horizon. A lilac line

cut between a cell-red blob.
Scans and scans of ocean
glass. The sky lowers on the star, turning
pink and moving slowly out of focus.

I WALK UP THE HILL BEHIND MY SECOND-FAVOURITE GRANDMOTHER'S HOUSE AND STARE AT A WHITE FRENCH TOWNHOUSE OVERGROWING WITH BOUGAINVILLEA, AND BEHIND THAT IS THE SEA, AND STREAMING FROM THE SEA IS A HUGE BRIGHT WIND, I AM HAPPY TO BE AWAY FROM YOU

The weather has been perfect.

LIMITLESS CINEMA

It's like the city just gives up.
And then the sea: winter flat, but hot.

A red wall on sand. A word
dragged out to the line.

We were describing the different ways we saw
the same thing.

Palm trees hanging in fog,
the unending heavy weather

where I came from.
I was always afraid

of drowning, I said
and filled my mouth with water.

This family is impossible, you said
my name over the grass.

Frangipanis plumed
a lukewarm perfume.

I felt the plastic of my phone turn sticky
in my hand. A softness fell between us.

It wasn't exactly beautiful. I spat
mouthfuls of water onto the beach.

FRAGRANTICA

I am in the world like an eyelid.
I open my mouth.
My voice leaves my body.
I kneel on the floor
pretending to be good. Sex
excites me then disgusts.
I kiss the man
I am falling in love with.
When a thing happens, nearby
objects become new. I work all day
selling perfume to people who are not famous.
What is the inverse
of ecstasy? I used to be in love
with crying. Rain falls into a bucket til I kick it down.
The world damages me, which is its right.
To assert opinion with fantasy
instead of reason. Mystery
is a state of wanting. Beauty
is harm's cellophane. A used anal swab
sits in my bag because the clinic
is shut. The most gorgeous thing about a person is that
you are not your job.

EVERYBODY AT THE CHILDREN'S PEACE
TOWER WANTS YOU TO BE HAPPY

The trees gave me shade, and their elegant
brunette silence.
The park was just gravel. I came here
alone. I looked at a toilet in a round
beautiful building. Wet
sand smeared ground
I walked on. For months
I examined my hysteria
with curiosity, gentle
to remind myself be patient don't
die just because
you want to. When I was a child
I saw an ad for toothpaste
that made me believe
magic is real.
There is fruit
on the trees. Here
cats sleep on graves
a kid's shirt says
dreamy cute existence. It is
that. And the rest. I'm grateful
for the experience of destroying
something that was mine. Real life
as they call it. Here
is my earring, my cool bag,
my cutthroat
calm. The thistle blooming on
my shirt. You have to
choose what you are in order to transcend it.

BOUNDARIES AGAINST INVINCIBILITY

*I do these / Things which I do, which please / No one
but myself* — Marianne Moore

It's a Monday in my life.
I'm a gay guy saying nothing

by talking for hours.
We are each our own god,

my friend says. A statement
I have no interest in. His earlobes

hang from his beautiful earrings
like pulled rope. I'm lonely

most days, I think more about shopping,
a cheap dinner, turning crueller in my taste.

The book is nearly done, and I have time
to stand each night in wet concrete.

The perfume of my newly-washed
apartment stairwell,

considering an absent god. I don't want
power, I want to win.

SUMMER MAKES US ALL THE SAME TYPE OF CRAZY

Larpers pose in a field.
My banana falls on the road.

The red tail light of a bike glows
on plants I don't know the names of.

A man hoses down
the tennis court beside the train.

It snakes by, freighting one
sleeping passenger. I watch

a mattress fold against a bush.
Confetti falls out a bedroom window.

I walk on grass. Oh god, this patience is all
I need to be happy.

A swan boat passes an identical swan boat.
Their necks make the shape of a heart in my mind.

LIGHT FILM

I fired
an arrow in
your peppermint mirror
like cream
on a knife
you left this
thistle on my shore
where I loved you
is a place
I looked at a rock
I heard a ringing bell
it grew dark over the water
then it grew dark over the ground

Notes

The following films/novels were used as writing prompts, and in some cases performed as thematic guides and/or titles for poems in this book.

Sebastiane (1976) Derek Jarman

Mirror (1975) Andrei Tarkovsky

Teorema (1968) Pier Paolo Pasolini

Paradise (1984) Ishu Patel

Rabbit's Moon (1972) Kenneth Anger

Knife + Heart (2018) Yann Gonzalez

Jordan's Dance (1977) Derek Jarman

Peppermint Frappé (1967) Carlos Saura

The Hour of the Star (1985) Suzana Amaral, adapted from the novel (1977) by Clarice Lispector

Querelle (1982) Rainer Werner Fassbinder, adapted from the novel *Querelle of Brest* (1947) by Jean Genet

Un Chant d'Amour (1975) Jean Genet

August in the Water (1995) Gakuryū Ishii

My Very Beautiful Movie (1974) Derek Jarman

Agatha et les Lectures Illimitées (1981) Marguerite Duras

Acknowledgements

Earlier versions of the poems *Jordan's Dance, 1977* and *Fire Island* were originally commissioned by Gus Fisher Gallery, Auckland, as part of the exhibition *Derek Jarman: Delphinium Days* (2024).

An earlier version of the poem *Narcissus Looks for Work* was published by Going Down Swinging as part of their comic-poem series, in collaboration with the artist Nick Mullaly. Thank you Nick, for this and other things.

The poem *Mirror, 1975* is included in the anthology *Wish the Whale Bell to be Made Fresh*. Thanks to Rachel Corry.

A selection of these poems were published in Landfall.

The poem *It is, after all, impossible to be taken seriously* borrows its title and opening line from the poem *Is it So Impossible to be Taken Seriously*, in my book *In the Printed Version of Heaven*, published by Rabbit, 2023.

Thank you to Richard Porter at Pilot Press for taking on this manuscript, and for your care in working on it with me. Thank you to Elaine Kahn and Poetry Field School, for reading and workshopping these poems with me. Thank you also to readers of earlier versions of this manuscript: Rafael Buck, Bonnie Harvey, Melinda Bufton, Ben Fama, and Lucinda Strahan.

Thank you to my family and my friends.

ISBN: 978-1-0687586-2-1

Published in the U.K. by Pilot Press